WATERSHED   **Teachers & Pupils**

Watershed

Published by: The Artists Archives of the Western Reserve
to accompany the Exhibition of the same name

Designed by: Mindy Tousley
Contributors include:
William Martin Jean
Ruth Bercaw
Thomas Roese
Ken Nevadomi
George Kozmon
Susan Donovan Lowe
Glen Ratusnik
Nick Taylor

All photography is courtesy of the artists or their agents

Support staff:
AAWR *Executive Director*: Mindy Tousley
AAWR *Archives Assistant* Christine Ries

AAWR Board:
Herbert Ascherman *Board President*
David Joranko *Vice President*
Jocelyn Ruf *Secretary*
Philip Bautista *Treasurer*

Richard Cline
Lee Heinen
Lauren Marchaza
Dr. Vincent Monnier
Stuart Pearl
John Sargent
Rota Sackerlotzcky

WATERSHED
Teachers & Pupils

November 12—December 19, 2015

Teachers: Ruth B. Bercaw, William Martin Jean,
Thomas R. Roese,

Pupils: Dexter Davis, Derek Hess, George Kozmon,
Susan Donovan Lowe, Ken Nevadomi, Glen Ratusnik,
Nick Taylor

Presented by
The Artists Archives of the Western Reserve
1834 E 123rd St., Cleveland Ohio 44106

Cover image: Ruth Bercaw   *Invitation*   mixed media on canvas   45" x 41"

The Artists Archives of the Western Reserve (AAWR) is a unique archival facility created to preserve representative bodies of work by Ohio visual artists.

Through ongoing research, exhibition, and educational programs the AAWR actively documents and promotes this cultural heritage for the benefit of the public.

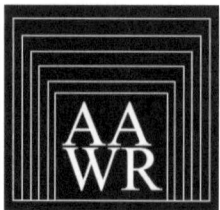

Curators Statement

Deciding on a career as an artist is seldom a " Eureka Moment" but there are little things along the way that point us in that direction; an elementary teacher putting your artwork on the display board, the poster contest where you won an honorable mention and the key award in the Scholastic Art Competition. All of these little things give you confidence and a sense of pride and makes your parents realize that they're sitting on a powder keg of creative potential.

All of the artists exhibiting here have similar stories to tell about how they came to the realization of pursuing a career as an artist. My high school art teacher was a Sister of Charities nun who made us understand that to become an artist you had to work at it seriously. It just wasn't something you did at school in art class, you had to do it all the time at home, think about it in church, read about it in libraries; look at art in museums, in magazines and books, and relate it to your other subjects. In other words it was total absorption that would make you stand out from the crowd.

Sister expected us to show up in the art room to work on holidays and summers were there to create a body of work that might be good enough to include in our portfolio for art school or college entrance.

" Watershed" includes three teachers Ruth Bercaw, Tom Roese and myself ,all of whom are also archived artists along with some of their former students who they taught in high school or in Saturday or summer programs or in colleges or universities. The background of each of these teachers is similar to mine in that there was someone early on who made them understand that there must be a total commitment if one is to succeed in this difficult business.

The development of an artist's work goes in many directions with many influences along the way. Sometimes these influences come early In an artist's career and sometimes later. We as teachers have the delightful and challenging task of attempting to open the eyes of young talent to the basic fundamentals of art and allow them to find their own creativity. Under our guidance, there may have been a turning point, a watershed moment, when the world of art opened up to them. These moments are difficult to pinpoint, but when they do, a certain energy develops feeding that talent into a satisfying personal pursuit.

Viewing the exhibition makes one aware that each of these of the artists has, in time found their own voice, creating diverse approaches in subject and media. It is always a proud moment when teachers can reflect on the part of the road that they helped these former students travel.

William Martin Jean 2015

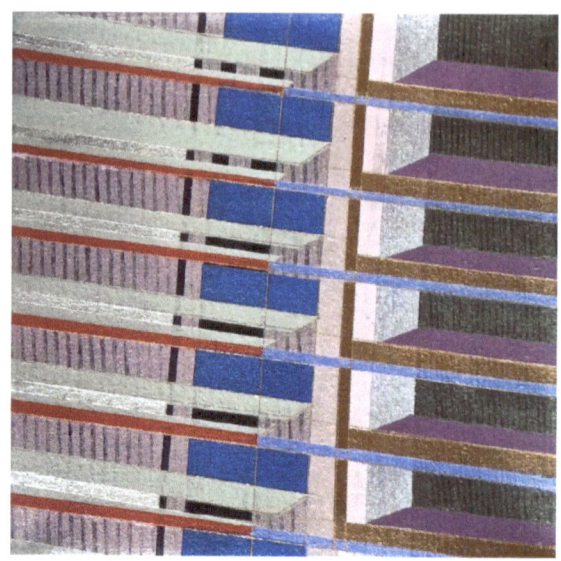

Louvre Series 3D 12 x 12" acrylic on canvas

WILLIAM MARTIN JEAN

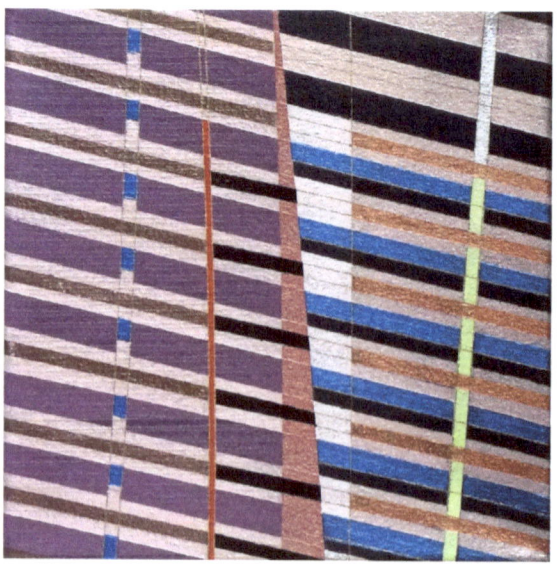

Louvre Series G 12 x 12" acrylic on canvas

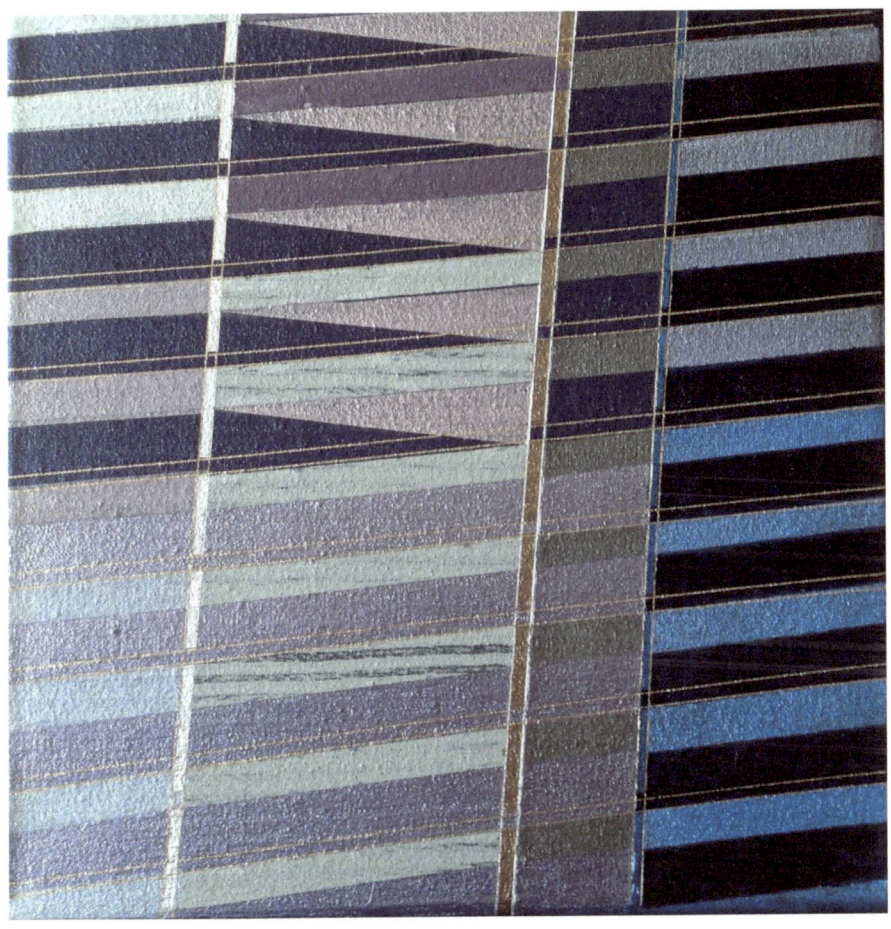

Louvre Series B   12 x 12" acrylic on canvas

RUTH B. BERCAW

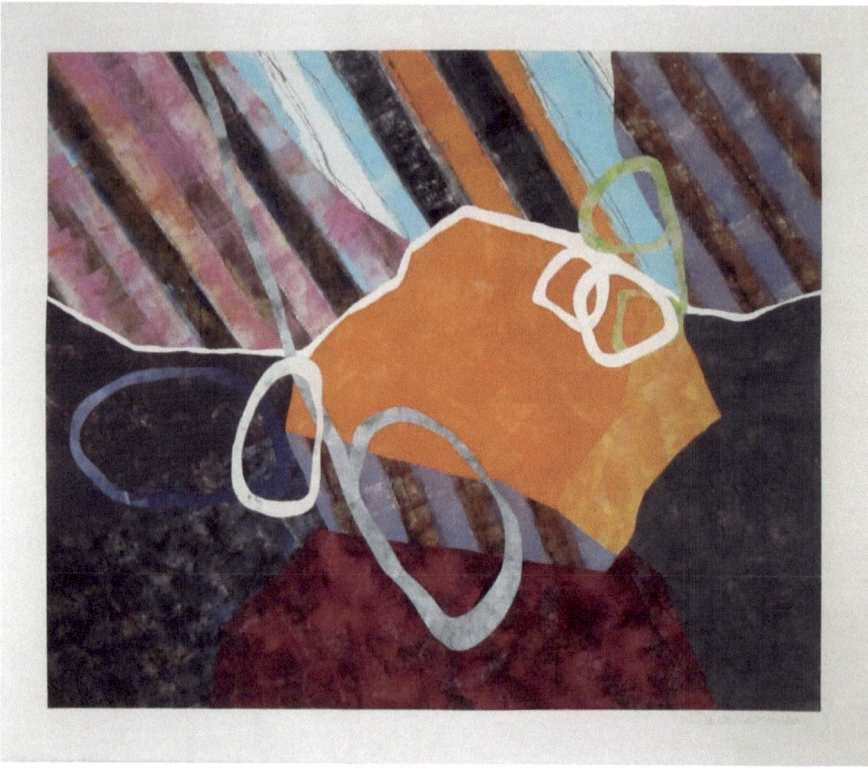

Venue   42" x 50" paper size   mixed media on paper

My teaching career dropped over my shoulders like a warm coat in the midst of a winter storm. I had just received a wonderful degree from a fine university, but I did not exactly have a plan for my future other than painting. The sun must have been out and shining brightly the day I was recommended by the university to teach drawing and painting to a small group of nascent artists. At the time, I had no notion that I would love being with students and enjoy teaching so much. I was effective in helping students set suitable goals and solve problems, so opportunities to teach college foundation classes repeatedly came my way.

 Beneath that flow of successes, however, there lurked a small distraction. Steeped as I had been in the mighty principles of high art, breaking from established rules of how to accomplish those exalted ends was difficult, and teaching them doubled the difficulty of breaking them when creating my own art. So, when my pent-up ideas later erupted, they arrived in an outpouring of abstractions. Indeed there were consistent elements in the outflow, among them a penchant for examining relationships; relationships of the very Waters to solid earth, of humans and creatures to each other, but also color.

"Invitation" and "Venue", both shown in WATERSHED, are examples of recent mixed media works which come out of observations of a small segment of wild nature, existing and succeeding where other such elements have forever come and gone. Gnarled oaks guard their territories, and sycamore trees draped with Virginia creepers lean out over a small creek edged with rushes and dragon flies flitting about. There is nothing remarkable about the features of the area I come from in Missouri. Not the limestone bluff or the small spring bubbling out from under it, not the thickets of undergrowth or blackberry brambles. But there is something like magic about the way it all fits together when the slanting rays of sunlight encounter the clutter of everything, creating stuttering strips of shade and puddles of warmth amidst cool darks. Small sketches, which I make on location, later trigger recollections in my studio. The sketches are the simplest of reminders, but they seem to insist that I reflect upon the interdependence of just about everything about us, and taken together, these things inspire my art.

It is clear that in my own work, I prefer making bold statements and leaving them to hang out in space, asking unanswerable questions about where, or why. No matter the daily grim news, I feel optimistic that sparks of varied life will survive unending eliminations and journey on, maybe even prosper. So here we all are, tiny specks in a vast universe, poised to skip along. Just being alive, and knowing it, is cause for celebration. And probably that's what my paintings are about: celebration.

Ruth B. Bercaw

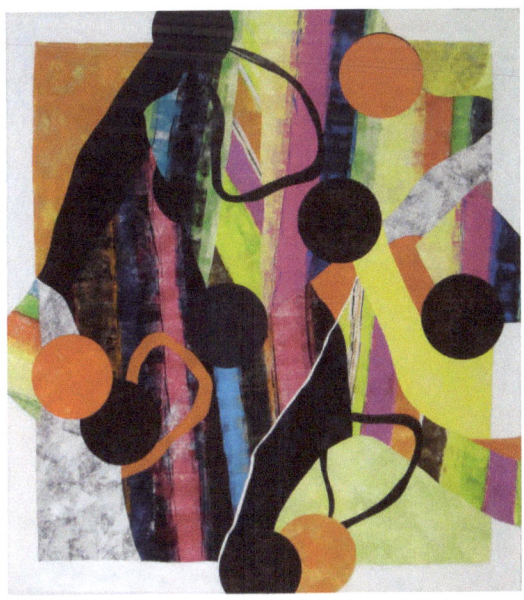

Invitation   45" x 41"   mixed media on canvas

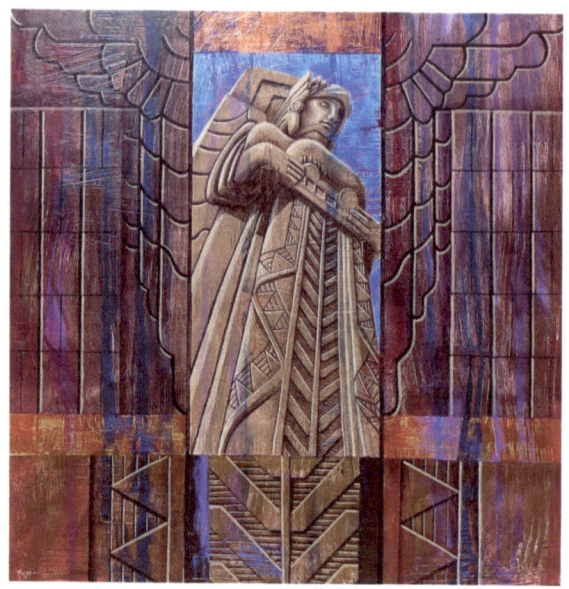

CL Detail Series WSM   30 x 30"   acrylic on canvas

THOMAS R ROESE

CL Detail Series H   30 x 30"   acrylic on canvas

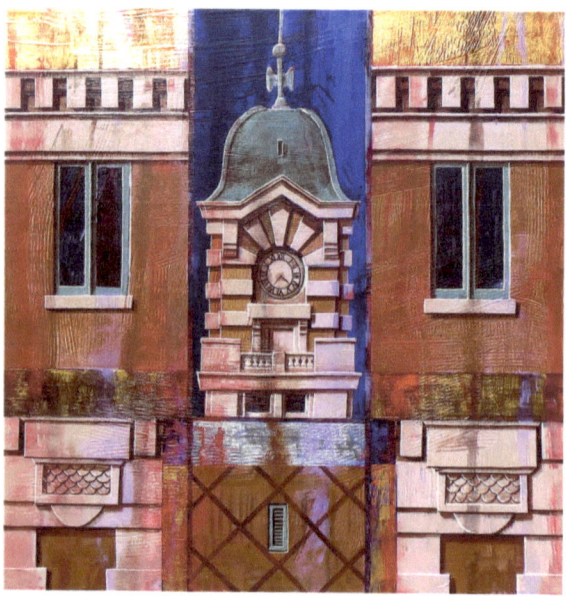

A career, like a life, is a journey. One chooses a path, experiments with a process, explores a new direction. During a long career, there may be many transitions.

As I travel the world, and compare the visual riches of other metropolitan landscapes and paradise-like rural venues, I am compelled to return time and again to Cleveland and other urban architectural and industrial gems.

Where can one find a better relationship between pattern, texture, light, and space as well as social sensibility than through the visual study of architecture? Whether that exploration is by means of very naturalistic painted imagery, or drawing which emphasizes pattern and texture, as well as realism.

The work for Watershed, demonstrates transition. Transition in one's own work, transition in teaching styles, transition in learning; these paintings represent all of these elements. This body of work served as a transition from one large body of work, to another; from painting architectural subjects in a naturalistic style, then work with textural/patterned components, all leading to combinations of these elements in current work.

Thomas R. Roese

CL Detail Series H   36 x 36"   acrylic on canvas

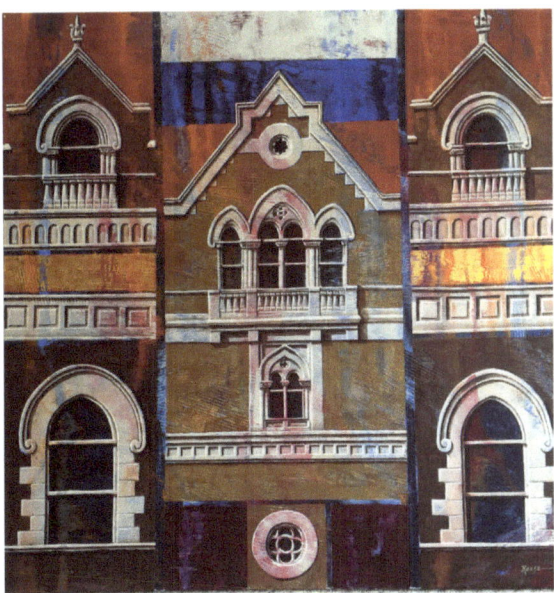

DEXTER DAVIS
Pupil of William Martin Jean

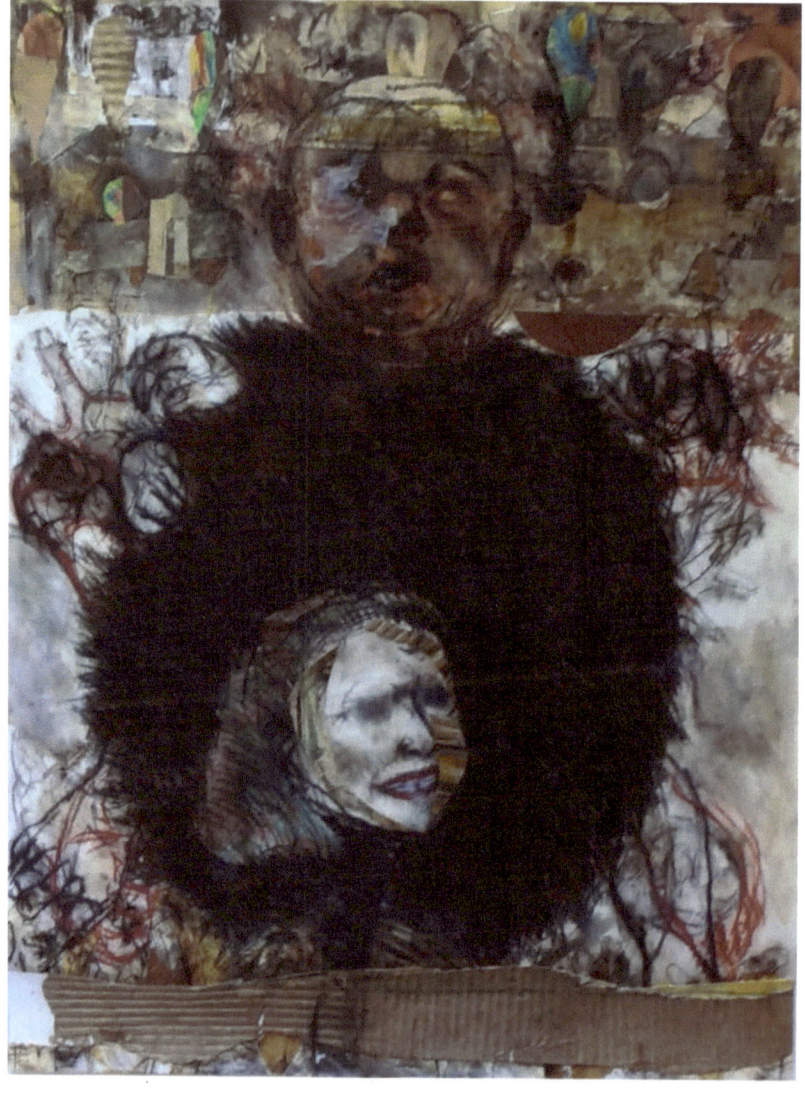

Untitled   52 x 40"   mixed media

DEREK HESS
Pupil of Ruth Bercaw

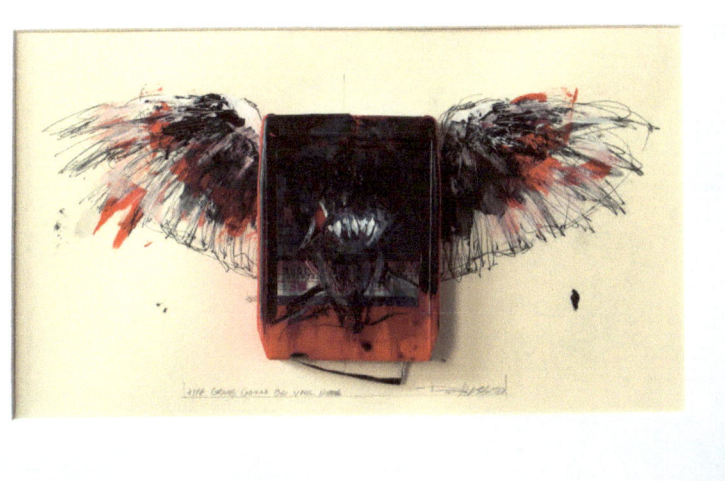

The Graves Gonna Be Your Home   14.5" x 21"   mixed media   8 track cassette

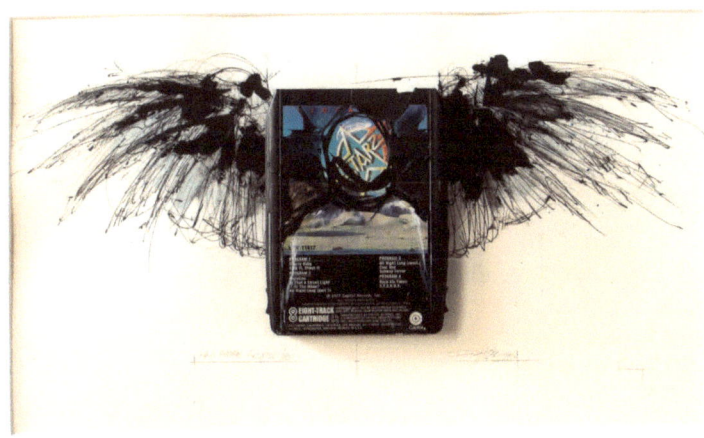

You Were so Polite   14.5" x 21"   mixed media,   8 track cassette

KEN NEVADOMI
Pupil of Ruth Bercaw

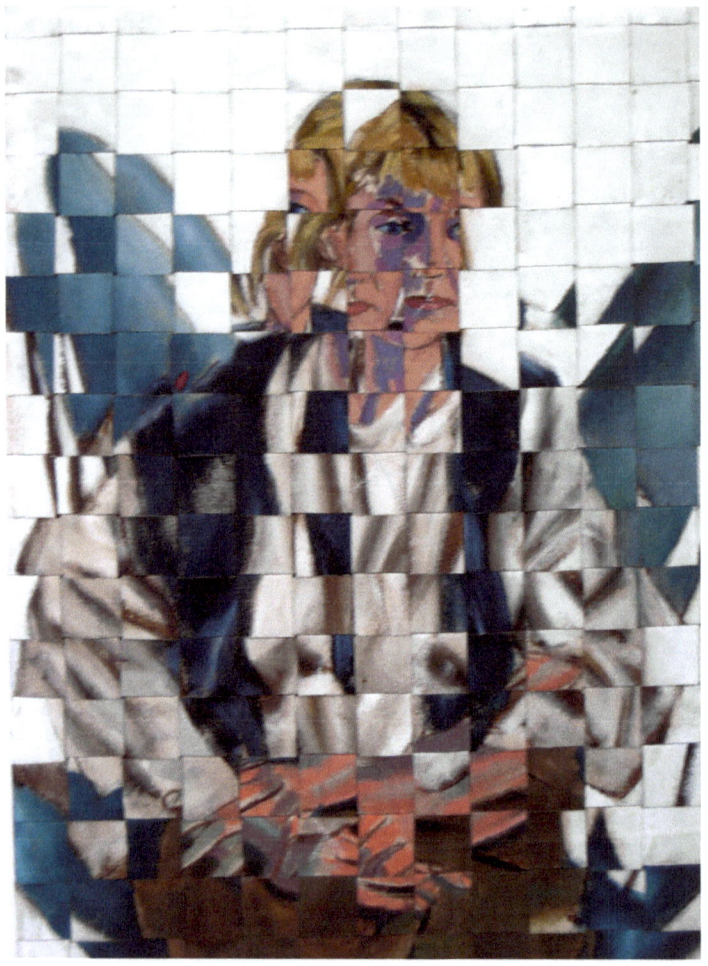

Portrait of Caroline Anderson   28.5 x 22"   mixed media

I was born in 1939 in Cleveland Ohio. Joined the military when I was 17 with the intension of making it a career. While in the service I discovered I could paint as well as draw. It was an 'epiphany' for me. When my hitch was up I went to art school.

I went to the Cooper School of Art In Cleveland for 2 years, Columbus College of Art and Design for a year and a half and Kent State for a masters degree. At Cooper I met Ruth Bercaw, one of the teaching faculty. She showed me painting wasn't a bunch of exercises. Rather, it was an adventure. She was an inspiration to me as an artist and teacher.She was an inspiration to me as an artist and teacher.

After Kent I was hired by Cleveland State U as painting and drawing instructor. A requirement was 'research'. In the art department this meant having art shows on a regular basis. I had one person and group shows as well as competitive art contests. I received several grants from the state of Ohio that helped further my career.

I'm retired now but still painting. And, buy the way, so is Ruth Bercaw

Ken Nevadomi

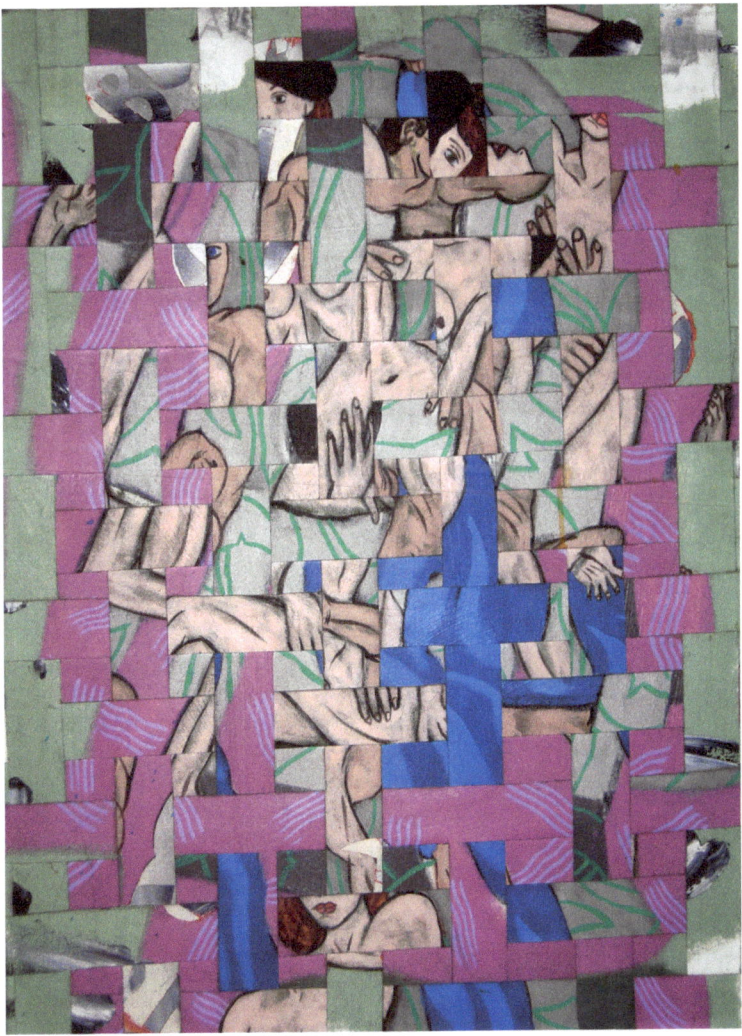

Osmosis   *28.5" x 22"*   mixed media

GEORGE KOZMON
Pupil of William Martin Jean

The Mountain Series of drawings, paintings, and digital explorations, focuses on the primal, inorganic, alpine landscape as metaphor, geological time and place beyond personal or general human scale. Images of landscapes affect us both physically and psychologically. They resonate with genetically encoded instincts that we aren't conscious of. The physical landscape is the provider of the heritage of human needs, a reminder of humans' fragility and vulnerability.

Many works incorporate symbols, variations of plus and minus signs. Metal-leaf (gold, silver) has a connotation of value; I'm gilding the landscape.

The stark images are developed with ink, acrylics, and hand-ground maple charcoal. Some materials reflect humanity's interaction with the environment: for charcoal I cut down trees, split them to size, burn them in my stove, hand-grind the remaining solid chunks of charcoal into a fine powder. This is contrasted by my interest in using digital technology to explore image-making in ways previously unavailable.

George Kozmon

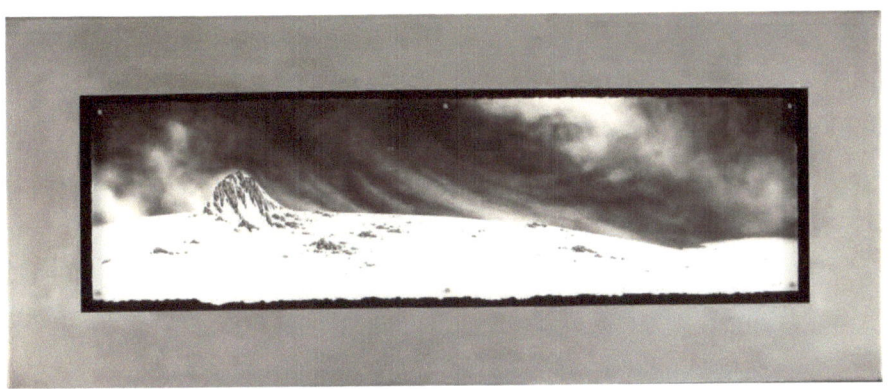

Outcropping   18" x 54"   ink, hand ground charcoal, paper and steel   2014

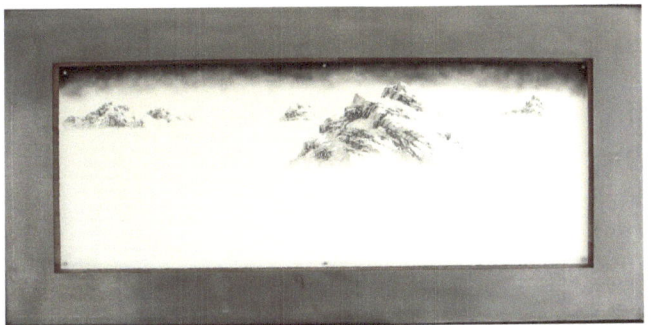

Emergent   22" x52"   ink, hand ground charcoal, paper and steel   2014

SUSAN DONOVAN LOWE
Pupil of Ruth Bercaw

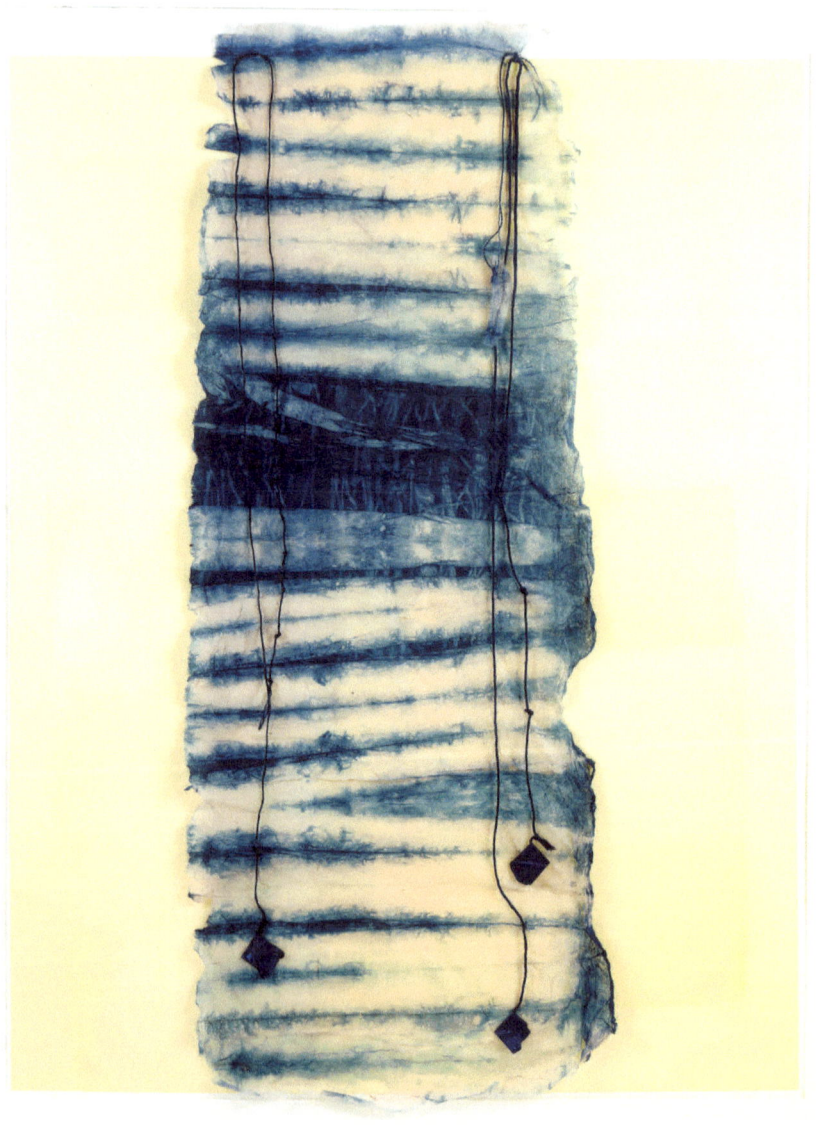

Paper Scroll   40" x 32"
indigo dyed hand made paper mounted on an oil painting

I am honored to have been invited to participate in this Watershed Exhibition. Thank you, Ruth, for being an outstanding mentor. Your guidance and example as an artist have totally inspired me through the years.

As a student at the Cleveland Institute of Art, I knew I loved color and saw beauty abundant in my surroundings. Ruth Bercaw, a visiting artist at CIA, was one of my first professors in painting. I vividly remember our beginning assignment in her class- to explore and play with color and bring the resulting color samples to class. The process was exhilarating and great fun. Ruth enthusiastically encouraged me to continue this discovery. Thirty years later, I am happy to say that I am still whole-heartedly following her advice. I usually feel best about the works that come out of this creative process, of exploring and embracing freedom and the surprise elements. Ruth taught me to enjoy and honor the doing while respecting the concept. Through many media: drawing, sculpture, collage, print, book arts, text, painting, and most recently handmade paper, I have used this approach.

Often my work begins with a glance and an emotional response to something visual. The process continues with a memory of the particular quality of grace or beauty that first attracted me. "Remembered Leaves" is just such a work. The sight is a sassafras tree I've watched from my window. I know it in all weathers. I've seen it as a seedling and now as a mature tree. I am intrigued by its variety of leaf shapes, clusters, and new growth. I've painted it both as I've observed it recently and as I remember it through the years. I began with a very dark palette of color, as seen in the frame. Then I layered it with very high key color, predominately white. Referring to its changes over time I scratched through the surface light to dark to reveal its first growth. The background outlines are its initial stems and sprouts. The ethereal atmosphere evokes its budding life force and physical history. The finished painting is a recognition of nature's perseverance, fragility, and energy through time. "Remembered Leaves" is my meditation on life's subtleties.

"Paper Scroll" is a mixed media piece with time and transparency as its subject. The indigo-dyed kozo paper is the result of my exploration this summer in the process of making and dyeing paper from local mulberry tree pulp. The monochromatic oil painted museum board backed grid painting is a reminder of a past pursuit. I explored the formal aspects of layering paint, paper, and object, and the use of translucency, shadow, and subtle color contrast to create space and indicate time. "Paper Scroll" is a contemplation of my current fortunes and my past experiences. Indeed, placing the two works together gave me the opportunity to merge the two media in an acknowledgement of both past art making and my current interests. When all is said and done, aren't we all this combination of past and present?

Susan Donovan Lowe

GLEN RATUSNIK
Pupil of Thomas Roese

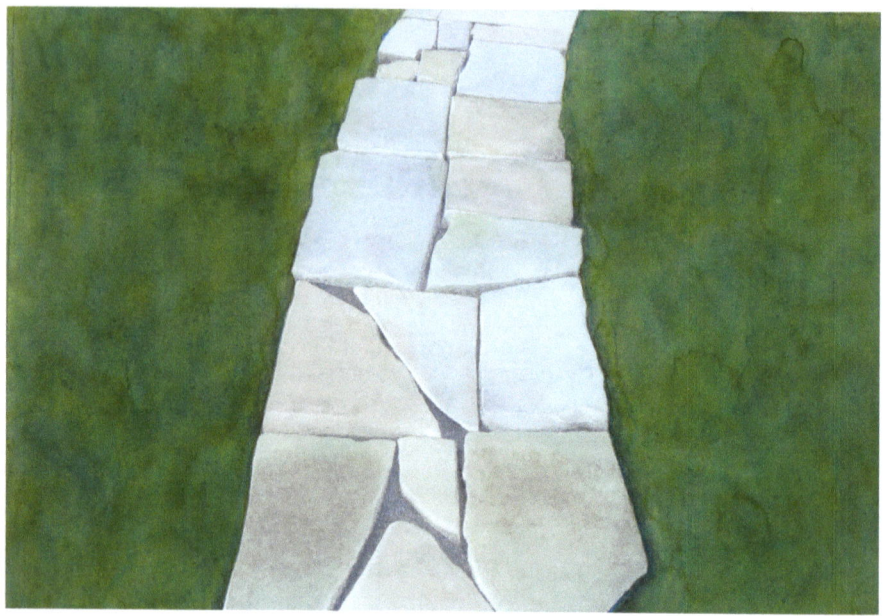

Untitled   8" x 10.5"   acrylic and graphite on vellum

I have lived in and around the Cleveland area for most of my life. And although I enjoy the city and the activity I need to be in touch with nature as well. I discovered Wendy Park through an interest in bird watching and found it to be an oasis in the middle of an industrial and urban environment. Its presence hints at the potential for a balance between the natural and human made worlds.

As an artist it is my job to achieve that same balance in my drawings with color and composition. I also find the act of art making to be meditative since it offers the opportunity to reflect. These drawings are mostly about the quiet time I've spent at the park.

Glen Ratusnik

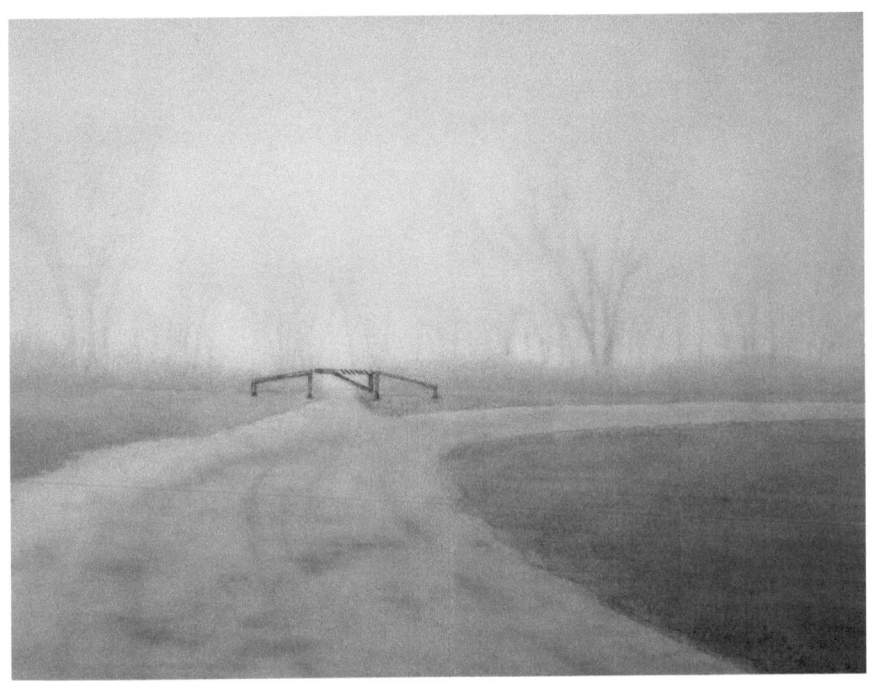

Untitled   8" x 10.5"   acrylic and graphite on vellum

NICK TAYLOR
Pupil of Thomas Roese

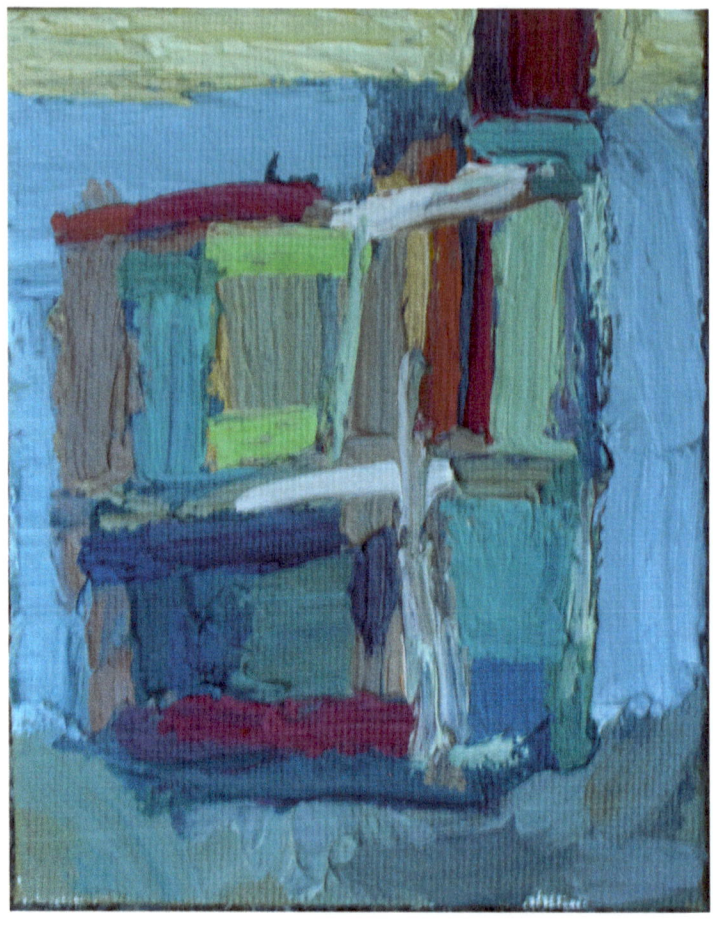

Untitled   4.875" x 4"   acrylic painting

These paintings are part of a continued series of small abstract landscapes that explore color theory and expressive passages of color. Every so often some sort of representation appears in the art work, a sign, a tree, a telephone poll; returning to the concrete/observed reality versus a cognitive/ theoretical one. This series, repetitive and continuous, constantly changes in color and mood but remains locked in a small rectangular format; a slight reference to the mass production in culture (and ironically nature) it tries to escape from by being a landscape.

Nick Taylor

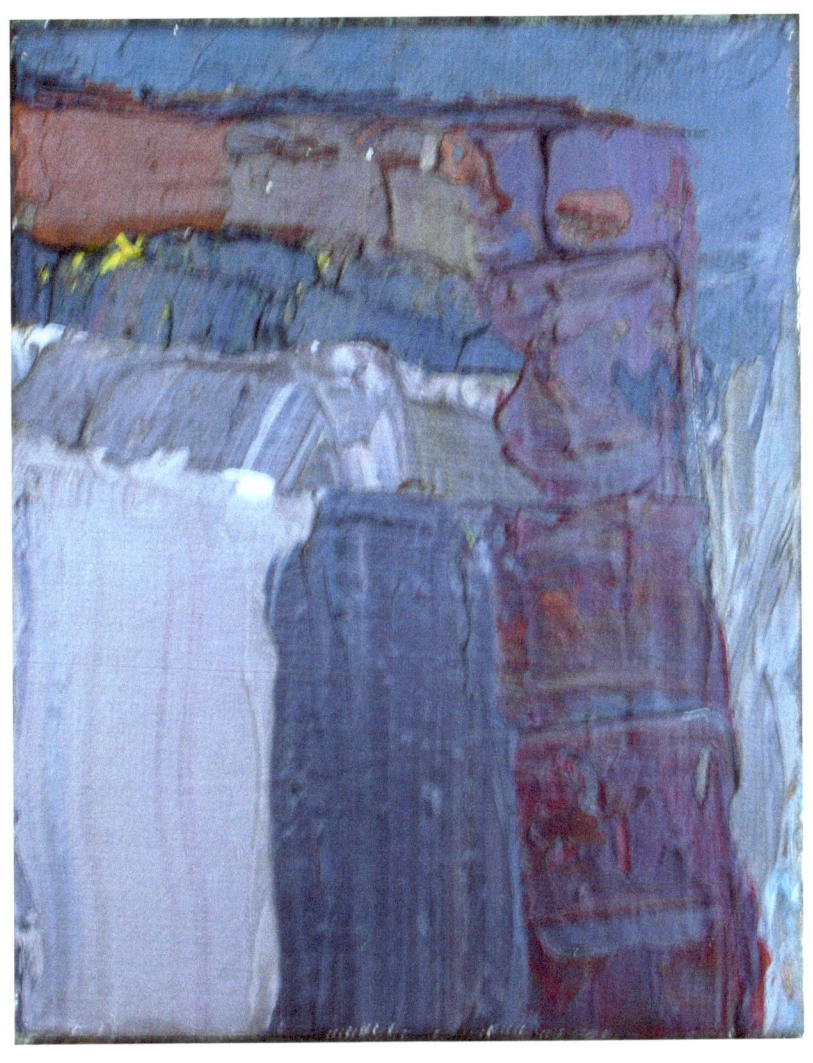

Untitled   4.875" x 4"   acrylic painting

www.ingramcontent.com/pod-product-compliance
Lightning Source LLC
Chambersburg PA
CBHW040916180526
45159CB00010BA/3097